I KNOW AMERICA

Our
Space
Program

Carmen Bredeson

THE MILLBROOK PRESS
Brookfield, Connecticut

Cover photograph courtesy of NASA

Photographs courtesy of UPI/Corbis-Bettmann: pp. 4, 16 (left), 19; Corbis-Bettmann:
pp. 6, 39; Corbis: pp. 9, 25; NASA: pp. 11, 13, 16 (right), 17, 18, 24, 26, 29, 31, 33,
35, 37, 38, 41, 43, 45; Tiziou/Sygma: p. 32

Library of Congress Cataloging-in-Publication Data
Bredeson, Carmen.
Our space program / Carmen Bredeson.
p.   cm. — (I know America)
Includes bibliographical references and index.
Summary: Examines the United States space program from the development of the first
rockets after World War II to the formation of NASA, the lunar landing, unmanned
space probes, and space stations of the future.
ISBN 0-7613-0952-7 (lib. bdg.)
1. Astronautics—United States—Juvenile literature. [1. Astronautics. 2. Outer space—
Exploration.] I. Title. II. Series.
TL793.B73   1999
629.4'0973—dc21   98-21693   CIP   AC

Published by The Millbrook Press, Inc.
2 Old New Milford Road
Brookfield, Connecticut 06804

5 4 3 2 1

INTRODUCTION

Since the beginning of human awareness, people have looked at the night sky in wonder. Many were mystified as they watched the moon appear to change shape. Some believed that the sun and moon were gods and worshiped them with songs and sacrifices. As the ages progressed, a few early astronomers began to record the patterns and movements they observed in the sky.

In 1609, Galileo Galilei helped to expand knowledge of the universe when he used a telescope to study the celestial bodies. Over time, larger and more powerful telescopes were built. By the 1950s, astronomers had collected huge amounts of information about the universe. One thing stood in the way of further knowledge, however, and that was Earth's atmosphere. The blanket of air that surrounds our planet filters out much of the light from space. It would be necessary to get above the atmosphere to see more clearly.

Experiments with rockets had been going on for many years. The gradual evolution of rocket science

A V-2 rocket is hoisted into place in New Mexico in 1946. The development of rockets in the United States and the Soviet Union signaled the beginning of the "space race" between the two countries.

5

This painting shows the young poet John Milton looking through Galileo's telescope. The older man with the beard is Galileo.

was pushed forward by World War II. German scientists developed the V-2 rocket, which was used to deliver bombs. After Germany lost the war, some of its scientists surrendered to the Americans and came to the United States to continue their work with the V-2 rockets. Other German scientists went to the Soviet Union, where they also used their knowledge to build and test rockets.

Tension developed between the United States and the Soviet Union during the years after World War II. Competition to see which country was stronger also led to a race to be the first in space. The Soviet Union took the lead in the "space race" when it put the first artificial satellite into orbit. America's space program quickly caught up to that of the Soviet Union and eventually won the race by landing astronauts on the moon. What followed was the beginning of a period of cooperation between the United States and the Soviet Union, now Russia, in matters related to space.

Today, science is the main emphasis of space exploration. Weather satellites, space shuttles, orbiting laboratories, and dozens of probes to the planets have all contributed to our knowledge of Earth and the universe.

The space missions of tomorrow will search even deeper for clues to the mysteries of our universe. Probes will explore the planets and their many interesting moons. Comets will also be investigated as they streak along, trailing their luminous tails. In the 21st century, there will be thousands of new things to study and for our space program to explore. The only problem will be in deciding where to begin.

CHAPTER

THE SPACE RACE

On October 4, 1957, Sputnik 1 was launched into orbit by the Soviet Union. The satellite was only the size of a big beach ball and weighed 184 pounds (84 kilograms), roughly the weight of a grown man, but it started the space race between the Soviet Union and its rival, the United States. Once every 96 minutes, the metal sphere circled the globe, beeping radio signals back to Earth. Traveling at a speed of 17,000 miles (27,370 kilometers) per hour, the successful launch of Sputnik 1 stunned the world!

Scientists and engineers in the United States were frustrated to have been beaten into space by the Soviets. Both countries had been working for years on rockets that were capable of carrying a satellite into orbit. There were many explosions and scrubbed (canceled) missions as rocket technology slowly developed. The United States was very close to a successful launch, but not quite close enough. With the word *zashiganiye*, which is Russian for "ignition," Sputnik 1 made history as the first man-made object to orbit Earth.

As the satellite passed over the United States, space scientists were not the only ones who watched in dismay. Military leaders also kept a close eye on the Soviet mission. For many years the Soviet Union and the United States had been involved in an arms race that was known as the Cold War. During this time, these two superpowers built bigger and more powerful weapons in an attempt to become the strongest military presence in the world. At the time, many believed that a massive arsenal of nuclear weapons served as a deterrent to an actual war.

The size of a large beach ball, Sputnik 1 began orbiting Earth on October 4, 1957. This Soviet photograph was taken just before its launch and shows Sputnik supported by a stand.

The successful launch of Sputnik 1 presented a whole new problem for the United States. If the Soviets were capable of launching a satellite into orbit, were they also able to deliver nuclear weapons from space? Developing the American space program became crucial for military as well as scientific reasons.

Nearly four months after the launch of Sputnik 1, the United States sent a bullet-shaped satellite called Explorer 1 into orbit. Weighing just 31 pounds (14 kilograms), the American satellite blasted into space on January 31, 1958. Its radio signals returned information to Earth about temperatures in space and cosmic rays.

The United States and the Soviet Union continued to send satellites into orbit during the next few years. Sputnik 3 spent 691 days in orbit beginning in 1958, and Sputnik 9 carried a variety of animals into space and returned them safely to Earth. Explorer 6 sent back the first television pictures of Earth in 1959, and Explorer 7 sent back radiation data about the sun from space. All of the Soviet and American missions were designed with one goal in mind: to learn enough to send a human being into orbit.

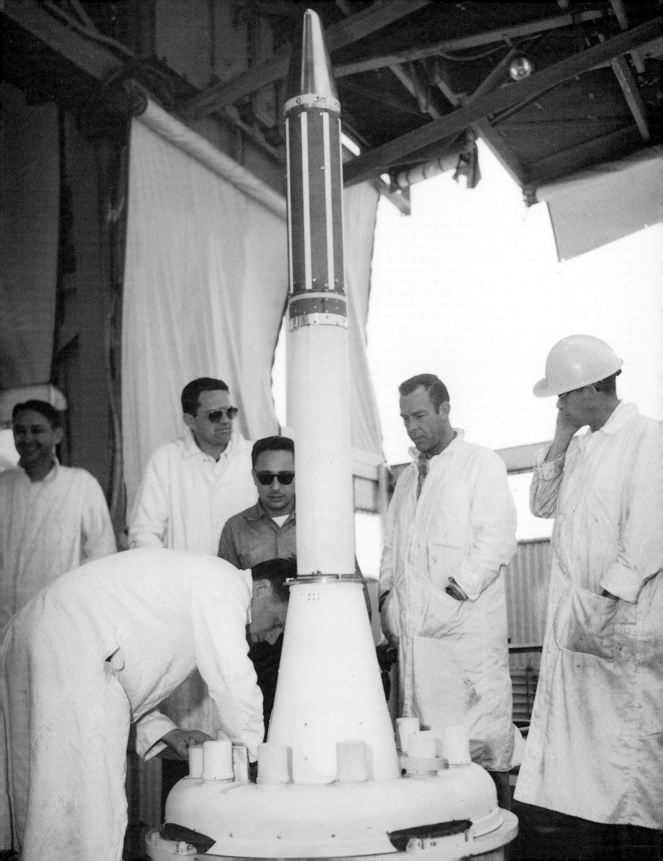

C H A P T E R

HUMAN SPACEFLIGHT

In 1958 the United States created the National Aeronautics and Space Administration (NASA). The agency began looking for volunteers who were willing to be blasted into space on top of blazing rockets. Each astronaut candidate had to have at least 1,500 hours of flying time, have test-pilot experience, and be less than 40 years old.

One hundred and ten military men met all of NASA's criteria, and they became the first astronaut candidates. There were no female test pilots in the military at the time, so no women were included in the group. After much physical and psychological testing, seven men were selected to become America's first astronauts. Their names were announced in a press conference on April 9, 1959.

They were:

Navy Lieutenant Malcolm Scott Carpenter

Air Force Captain Leroy Gordon Cooper

Marine Lieutenant Colonel John Herschel
   Glenn Jr.

Air Force Captain Virgil I. ("Gus") Grissom

Navy Lieutenant Commander Walter M. Schirra Jr.
Navy Lieutenant Commander Alan B. Shepard Jr.
Air Force Captain Donald K. Slayton

The men, who were known as the "Mercury Seven" because they would be flying in Mercury space capsules, were hailed as heroes by an adoring public. Their faces appeared in newspapers and magazines, while their words were repeated over and over on television and radio news programs. Most viewed the Mercury Seven as brave men who were willing to sacrifice their lives for the exploration of space.

Dressed in their space suits, the first astronauts selected by NASA posed for a picture in 1962. Front row, left to right: Schirra, Slayton, Glenn, Carpenter. Back row, left to right: Shepard, Grissom, Cooper.

Space exploration has led to the development of a great deal of new technology that has made our lives on Earth better and safer.

Fire Safety. Nearly everything that a firefighter wears today was developed from space suit technology. The thin, fire-resistant fabric of the suits along with effective breathing equipment were first designed for the Apollo astronauts so that they could work on the moon. In addition, smoke detectors that are now found in most homes and businesses were created to alert the Skylab crews of possible fires.

Weather Forecasting. The first true weather satellite, Tiros 1, was launched into orbit in 1960. Since that time, dozens of others have been sent into space to help monitor conditions on Earth. The satellites transmit data about weather patterns all over the world. In the past, hurricanes, floods, and blizzards struck with little warning. Today, alerts are broadcast so that people can prepare in advance for violent weather.

Athletic Shoes. When astronauts walked on the moon, they needed sturdy boots to protect their feet. Their boots contained a material that cushioned the feet and helped to keep them cool. Many athletic shoes and hiking boots today use that same kind of material to absorb shocks and reduce foot fatigue.

Other Spin-offs. Many other products have been developed as a result of space technology. Among them are heart-rate monitors, quartz crystal clocks and watches, freeze-dried food, shock-absorbing helmets, trash compactors, water purification systems, programmable heart pacemakers, voice-controlled wheelchairs, and aircraft-icing sensors.

As soon as the excitement surrounding their selection died down, the astronauts had to go to work and learn how to become spacemen. They were whirled around in a giant centrifuge to mimic the pressures their bodies would feel during liftoff and reentry. They also experienced weightlessness in the cargo hold of a transport plane as it rose and dipped sharply in the sky. Sometimes the plane repeated the maneuver more than 50 times in one flight, and some of the trainees got sick from the motion. When the astronauts were not being tossed around, they studied astronomy, flight operations, and emergency procedures.

The day finally arrived when NASA was ready to send a man into space. Alan Shepard was selected to be America's first astronaut, and his flight was scheduled for May 5, 1961.

Less than one month before Shepard's flight, Soviet cosmonaut Yuri Gagarin had blasted into space aboard Vostok 1, on April 12, 1961. He orbited Earth just one time before a successful reentry and landing. That one orbit, though, gave him the distinction of being the first human being in space. Once again the Soviet Union had beaten the United States in the space race.

Alan Shepard's flight lifted off as planned from Cape Canaveral, Florida. America's first astronaut did not go into orbit, but made a successful 15-minute suborbital flight. The United States was back in the race! After Shepard's flight, President John F. Kennedy made a speech in which he said, "I believe this nation should commit itself to achieving the goal, before this decade is out, of landing a man on the Moon and returning him safely to Earth."

NASA and the country were taken by surprise. The United States had not even put an astronaut into orbit, and Kennedy was talking about going to the moon in

Above left: Yuri Gagarin of the Soviet Union was the first person to travel in space. He orbited Earth once in his ship Vostok 1 before safely reentering Earth's atmosphere.

Above right: Astronaut Alan B. Shepard Jr. prepares to be the first American to travel in space. His 15-minute suborbital flight put the United States back in the space race.

less than ten years! NASA readied itself for the challenge and was allocated $1.7 billion by Congress to begin the hard work that would be necessary to achieve Kennedy's goal. The technology would have to be developed in stages, each one building on the last, with astronaut safety always the main concern.

If NASA were to meet Kennedy's challenge, it needed more room to work than it had at its facilities in Virginia and Florida. After considering several possible sites, Houston, Texas, was chosen as the location for the Manned Space Center (MSC). It would contain the command center and the astronaut training facilities, as well as NASA's medical, engineering, and scientific departments. All missions would be directed from Houston after they lifted off from Cape Canaveral, Florida.

JOHN GLENN

On February 20, 1962, John Glenn became the first American astronaut to orbit Earth. He made the three-orbit flight in Friendship 7, a one-man Mercury capsule. In 1998, 36 years after his historic flight, John Glenn was named as a crew member on a space shuttle mission. At 77 years of age, Glenn will be the oldest human being to travel in space.

As part of his training, Glenn was whirled around in a centrifuge, which simulates the pressure astronauts feel during liftoff and reentry. During the two, 8½-minute spins, he was hooked up to a heart monitor, which measured the effects of the ride on his physical condition. He passed the test with flying colors.

During the ten-day miss... John Glenn, who is also ...ed States senator from O'... erved as a payload speciali... duties included studying ... effects of

weightlessness on the human body. Living in weightlessness promotes bone loss, muscle weakness, and loss of balance, problems that also

President John F. Kennedy and astronaut ...Glenn look through the porthole of ...e Mercury space capsule in which Glenn orbited Earth. Glenn is wearing a medal that was presented to him by the president.

affect some elderly people on Earth. Glenn hoped that tests conducted on him will help provide information on the aging process.

While NASA was hard at work, the Soviet space program was also sending cosmonauts into orbit. Voskhod 1 carried three Russians on a 15-orbit flight of

Earth in 1964, and during Voskhod 2, a Soviet cosmonaut made the first space walk in 1965. Competition continued between the two countries, but by the end of the Gemini program, American astronauts had spent more total time in space than the Russian cosmonauts. The next stop for the United States would be the moon!

C H A P T E R

SHOOT FOR THE MOON!

While the Gemini program was still in progress, NASA began sending unmanned probes to investigate the lunar (moon) surface. More needed to be learned about the conditions on the moon before astronauts could go there. In 1964, Ranger 7 transmitted more than 4,000 pictures of the moon before crash-landing onto the surface. They were the first close-up pictures of the moon ever seen by those living on Earth.

In 1966, Surveyor 1 made a soft landing on the moon and returned over 10,000 pictures to Earth. Surveyor 3 scooped up samples of the lunar soil and sent pictures of the samples back to NASA scientists. Five Lunar Orbiters also circled the moon during 1966 and 1967. The photographs that they sent back to NASA were used to choose the actual landing sites for the upcoming Apollo missions.

As the program got under way, many steps had to be completed before a moon landing could be attempted. The first step was a test of the Apollo capsule.

It was cone-shaped, just like the Mercury and Gemini capsules, but was designed to hold three astronauts. During moon landings, two astronauts would descend to the lunar surface in the lunar module(LM) while one remained in orbit in the command module.

Apollo 1 astronauts were scheduled to test the capsule in Earth's orbit in February 1967. A month before the mission, a practice run of the countdown was being conducted when a fire broke out in the capsule. All three astronauts died in the blaze, and the manned Apollo program came to an abrupt halt. During the next 21 months, the fire was investigated and many safety features were added to the Apollo capsule to make it safer for future missions. While the capsule was being redesigned, three unmanned Apollo missions were flown to test equipment and procedures.

Finally, on October 11, 1968, Apollo 7 blasted into space carrying three astronauts. They spent 11 days in Earth's orbit, testing guidance and control systems, space suits, and food. Two months later, Apollo 8 lifted off for the moon carrying astronauts Frank Borman, James Lovell, and William Anders. On Christmas Eve 1968, they became the first human beings to orbit the moon. After ten orbits, the main engine was fired, and Apollo 8 began its return to Earth. It splashed down safely in the Pacific Ocean on December 27, 1968.

The historic flight of Apollo 8 put the proposed moon landing back on track. Two more manned missions were flown to further test the equipment before Apollo 11 lifted off on July 16, 1969, for a rendezvous with the lunar surface. As the Saturn V rocket carrying the spacecraft *Columbia* belched smoke and flames,

On January 27, 1967, astronauts Gus Grissom, Edward White, and Roger Chaffee ate lunch and then put on their space suits. They climbed into the Apollo 1 spacecraft, which was perched on top of a Saturn V rocket at Cape Canaveral, Florida. This was just a practice session, staged to check out the first capsule in the Apollo program. The real liftoff would take place a month later.

The door was sealed and the capsule was filled with pure oxygen, just as it would be during the actual flight. For hours the astronauts checked their instruments and practiced procedures. After five hours of testing, one more countdown was started. Scientists and technicians in the control center watched the astronauts over closed-circuit television.

With just ten minutes left in the countdown, someone shouted "Fire!" Those in the control center watched in horror as flames filled the monitor's screens. The pad crew raced to get the hatch door open, but were driven back by an explosion. Six minutes after the fire started, the door was finally pried open. Everything inside was burned black. The astronauts' suits had protected them from the flames, but not from the toxic fumes. All three astronauts died in the blaze.

The manned Apollo program was delayed for nearly two years while the tragedy was investigated. It was determined that a wire short-circuited under Grissom's seat and started the fire. Later Apollo flights used a combination of mixed gases instead of pure oxygen, which fed the fire too well. Also, the hatch door was redesigned so that it could be opened in just a few seconds from inside, instead of the 90 seconds needed for the old hatch.

thousands watched from the roads and beaches surrounding Cape Canaveral, Florida. They cheered as Neil Armstrong, Buzz Aldrin, and Michael Collins embarked on one of mankind's greatest adventures.

The successful Apollo 11 mission was manned by astronauts Neil A. Armstrong, Michael Collins, and Edwin E. "Buzz" Aldrin Jr.

After circling Earth one and a half times, an engine fired to propel *Columbia* on a path to the moon. The astronauts raced through the blackness of space for three days before being pulled into orbit by the moon's gravity. On their fifth day in space the lunar module, *Eagle*, undocked from *Columbia* and descended to the surface of the moon. As *Eagle* flew lower and lower, Neil Armstrong realized that they were headed right for a crater that was full of huge rocks.

Armstrong took manual control of the lunar module and started to look for a safer place to land. As the seconds ticked by, *Eagle's* fuel supply got dangerously low. Buzz Aldrin had his hand on the abort button as Armstrong scanned the terrain. If the fuel level got too low, the mission would have to be scrubbed. Ninety seconds worth of fuel became 45 and then 30 seconds. Finally, with less than 20 seconds of fuel remaining, *Eagle* radioed to NASA: "Houston, Tranquility Base here. The *Eagle* has landed."

Once safely on the lunar surface, the astronauts checked all of their instruments, rested, and began the long process of putting on their space suits. Then they opened *Eagle's* hatch, and Neil Armstrong began a historic trip down the ladder. As he became the first

grams) of moon rocks, pebbles, sand, and dust was returned to Earth by the astronauts. The samples were taken to NASA's Lunar Laborator n Houston, Texas, where they are still studied tod As technology continues to improve, new things are constantly being learned from the lunar material.

CHAPTER

SPACE SCIENCE

After the space race slowed down, the United States and the Soviet Union embarked on a period of better relations. Each country continued to develop its space program, but the intense need to outmaneuver the other was gone. America put the space station Skylab into orbit in 1973, where it remained until 1979.

The Soviet Union also placed several Salyut space stations into orbit during the 1970s. Various problems plagued the early stations. It was not until Salyut 6 and 7 that longer stays in space were achieved by the cosmonauts. While aboard the stations, the Soviets conducted scientific research, set space endurance records, and welcomed guest cosmonauts who visited from other countries. No American astronauts spent time aboard Salyut, but the Soviet Union and the United States did arrange a meeting in space.

On July 15, 1975, a Soyuz spacecraft lifted off in Russia, followed about seven hours later by the liftoff of an Apollo spacecraft in America. Two days later a successful docking was completed, and the astronauts

Five months after the last Apollo mission, the Skylab space station was launched, on May 14, 1973. During the next year, three teams of astronauts spent a total of six months aboard the orbiting laboratory. While on board they performed several space walks and studied things such as the comet Kohoutek and the sun.

The space station was also used to measure the effects of weightlessness on the human body as the Skylab astronauts spent gradually longer and longer periods in space. They exercised, tested food, and conducted experiments. Their successful missions helped prove that human beings could live in space for months at a time. The longest and final Skylab mission lasted nearly three months in 1974.

After the last crew left, the space station continued to circle Earth until 1979. Its orbit fell lower and lower, and Skylab reentered Earth's atmosphere on July 11, 1979. Parts of the space station that survived reentry fell on Australia and in the Indian Ocean.

This photograph of Skylab was taken by a command/service module that was inspecting the space station. Note the solar-paneled "wing," which extends from the top of the craft. There should be another on the opposite side, but it is completely missing.

entered a module that connected the capsules. The cosmonauts also entered the module and shook hands with the Americans. Television cameras relayed the historic meeting to viewers on Earth as it took place. During the two days that the Apollo and Soyuz capsules were docked, the crews visited back and forth and performed some joint experiments.

In the early 1970s, with the space race no longer an issue, the United States turned its attention to the development of a reusable spacecraft. The shuttle, as it would be known, would be launched just like other spacecraft, but would return to Earth and land like an airplane at the end of its mission. In the past, space capsules like those of the Mercury, Gemini, and Apollo programs were used only one time. Shuttles could be used over and over and would serve as orbiting laboratories for scientific research. Astronauts would also be able to launch satellites from the shuttle's cargo bay and repair broken or damaged satellites already circling Earth.

After ten years of work, NASA successfully launched the space shuttle *Columbia* on April 12, 1981. The first shuttle flight was designed to test the spacecraft and its equipment. After *Columbia's* maiden voyage, it flew four more missions before a second shuttle, *Challenger*, was launched. A third shuttle, *Discovery*, made its maiden voyage in 1984, and *Atlantis* joined the lineup in 1985. The United States now had four shuttles that were used for orbital missions around Earth.

A space shuttle can stay in orbit for about two weeks. During that time, the crews work long days conducting experiments, deploying satellites, taking photographs, and doing routine chores. The astronauts also have to spend a couple of hours a day exercising to keep their bones and muscles strong. On Earth, gravity pulls on the body, causing it to work harder. In space, the effects of gravity on the body are reduced so the

SPACE JUNK

There are many kinds of useful satellites circling Earth. Some transmit television and radio signals, while others relay telephone calls, E-mail messages, and banking information to all parts of the globe. In addition to the useful satellites there are thousands of pieces of "space junk" in orbit.

The Space Control Center, which tracks the debris, has identified more than 8,000 items that are at least 4 inches (10 centimeters)

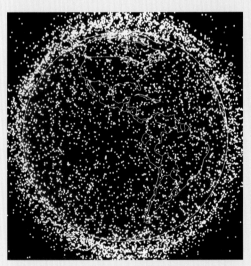

This is a computer-generated view of the thousands of satellites, used rocket stages, and other "space junk" orbiting close to Earth. Look carefully: You can see the outlines of North and South America.

long. Thousands more pieces of space junk are too small to track. Orbiting overhead are bolts and tools lost by spacewalking astronauts, pieces of old rockets, a camera lost by Michael Collins during Gemini 10, and even a glove that got away from Ed White, who performed the first American space walk in 1965.

While the smaller items might not seem like a threat to the huge space shuttle, imagine a bolt traveling at a speed of 17,000 miles (27,370 kilometers) per hour. It could shatter a satellite or punch a hole in the shuttle. A collision with a large piece of space junk could be disastrous. In 1991 an American shuttle had to change course quickly to avoid passing too close to pieces of a Soviet rocket.

Much of the space junk will eventually reenter the atmosphere and burn up. Occasionally some of the pieces survive reentry and crash-land somewhere on Earth as parts of Skylab did in 1979. As the area around Earth becomes more crowded, space junk could pose a real threat to astronaut safety.

bones and muscles do not have to work as hard. Regular exercise helps keep the bones from losing calcium and the muscles from shrinking.

Both men and women astronauts serve as crew members on shuttle flights. For twenty years, all NASA astronauts had been men. In 1978 the space agency decided that the shuttles required more variety among their crews. The orbiter pilots would still need to have intensive test-flight experience, but scientists, doctors, and engineers were also needed for many of the shuttle's other jobs. That opened the door for women astronaut candidates.

In 1978 the first six women astronauts were formally admitted to the program. They were Anna Fisher, Shannon Lucid, Judith Resnik, Sally Ride, Rhea Seddon, and Kathryn Sullivan. The women went through the same training as the men and were required to perform the same jobs. On June 18, 1983, Sally Ride became the first American woman in space on the *Challenger* STS-7 mission.

The first women astronauts, from left to right: Seddon, Fisher, Resnik, Lucid, Ride, and Sullivan.

Three years later, the space-shuttle program suffered a severe setback with the explosion of the space shuttle *Challenger* on January 28, 1986. Killed in the explosion were crew members Richard Scobee,

CHALLENGER DISASTER

January 28, 1986, dawned cold and clear at Cape Canaveral, Florida. Icicles hanging from parts of the launch tower sparkled in the bright sunshine. Friends of the astronauts, along with their family members, shaded their eyes as *Challenger* lifted off into the blue sky. Aboard were six astronauts and Christa McAuliffe, the first civilian school-teacher selected to fly in space.

Seventy-three seconds after liftoff, a solid rocket booster broke loose and smashed into *Challenger's* external liquid-fuel tank. An explosion and fireball ripped the space shuttle apart, sending it plunging into the Atlantic Ocean, while the dazed spectators watched in horror. All seven astronauts aboard *Challenger* were killed.

An investigation showed that the O-rings between two solid rocket booster sections had failed. Cold temperatures caused the material to become brittle so that it did not seal properly. Flames shooting out of the side of the booster cut through the support that attached the tank to the shuttle. When the solid rocket booster broke free it ruptured the liquid fuel tank, causing the explosion. There was not another shuttle flight for more than two years while NASA engineers redesigned the O-rings and implemented additional safety precautions for future shuttle flights.

The *Challenger* crew. Front row, left to right: Smith, Scobee, McNair. Back row, left to right: Onizuka, McAuliffe, Jarvis, Resnik.

Michael Smith, Ronald McNair, Ellison Onizuka, Judith Resnik, Gregory Jarvis, and Christa McAuliffe, the first civilian schoolteacher selected to fly in space. It would take two years of investigations before another shuttle lifted off into space.

A fifth shuttle, *Endeavour*, was added to the fleet in 1992, to replace *Challenger*. The four remaining shuttles continue to be operational and have flown dozens of missions. On a memorable mission that took place in 1990, the crew of *Discovery* launched the Hubble Space Telescope into orbit. With a 94.5-inch (240-centimeter) primary mirror, the telescope is capable of taking sharp pictures of space with no interference from Earth's atmosphere. Soon after launch, however, defects were discovered in the mirror and the pictures sent back by Hubble were fuzzy and out of focus.

The crew of *Endeavour* came to the rescue in December 1993. During a week of space walks, astronauts replaced two solar panels and installed two piano-size instruments that corrected Hubble's optical defect. The successful repair job resulted in spectacular pictures from the telescope.

Hubble was watching when more than 20 mountain-size fragments of the Shoemaker-Levy comet smashed into Jupiter in 1994. Some of the impacts shot fireballs 2,000 miles (3,220 kilometers) above Jupiter's cloud tops. The telescope has also photographed deep space, where thousands of galaxies formed. Their light is only reaching us now, billions of years later. Shuttle missions planned for 1999 and 2002 will upgrade the instruments and cameras on Hubble again, allowing them to see with even greater depth and clarity.

Astronaut F. Story Musgrave, anchored to the end of the Remote Manipulator System (RMS) arm, prepares to be raised to the top of the Hubble Space Telescope to do some work. Astronaut Jeffrey A. Hoffman (bottom of photograph) assisted him.

The other planets in our solar system were also in line for visits from NASA space probes. Mariner 10 completed one flyby of Venus in 1974 before using the gravity of that planet to propel it on toward Mercury. Mariner 10 was the first spacecraft to use this slingshot method of getting from one place to another in space. The technique is still used today in planetary exploration.

Additional missions to the planets included those of Pioneer 10 and 11, which were launched in 1972. They were the first space probes to visit the outer planets. On their trips to Jupiter and Saturn, Pioneer 10 and 11 also returned data about the asteroid belt, a 270-million-mile (485-million-kilometer) path between Mars and Jupiter. Within this area of space, thousands of asteroids can be found, some pebble-size and others that measure hundreds of miles in diameter. The safe trip of Pioneer 10 and 11 through the asteroid belt was a relief to scientists who were unsure whether such a passage was even possible.

As space exploration progressed, technology became more complex. The Voyager 1 and 2 probes weighed three times as much as the Pioneer spacecraft and sent information back to Earth at a faster rate. In the late 1970s, they sent back amazing images of Saturn's rings and moons before using the giant planet's gravity to hurl them toward Uranus and Neptune. After

Viking 1 recorded this color image of the surface and sky of Mars in 1976. Since the bright orange cord in the foreground was reproduced close to its true color, it was assumed that the red-orange color of the Martian rocks, soil, and sky was true, as well.

arriving at the far reaches of the solar system, Voyager 2 discovered six new moons of Neptune.

The expensive planetary probes of the first few decades of space exploration have given way to smaller, less expensive missions. Budgetary restraints have kept NASA from spending the amount of money that it had in the past. Scientists have had to design spacecraft that are less expensive to launch and operate.

Lunar Prospector, which was launched on January 6, 1998, weighed only 660 pounds (300 kilograms) and

MARS PATHFINDER

In the Jet Propulsion Laboratory in Pasadena, California, space scientists waited anxiously on July 4, 1997. As Pathfinder's first images of the red planet began to appear on the monitors, the scientists jumped to their feet and cheered, while the song "Twist and Shout," sung by the Beatles, blasted over the loudspeakers.

This view from Pathfinder shows Sojourner and a small part of the Martian landscape. The white forms on either side of Sojourner are air bags used to absorb the shock of landing on Mars.

The world also got to see the amazing pictures beamed back to Earth as Pathfinder's cameras scanned the Martian surface from 119 million miles (192 million kilometers) away. When the probe's solar panels parted like a flower opening its petals, a little rover named Sojourner could be seen nestled within. Looking much like a toy, Sojourner rolled down a ramp and started analyzing the rocks and soil in the Ares Vallis of Mars. All the world got to meet Martian rocks that the scientists gave playful names such as Yogi, Barnacle Bill, and Scooby-Doo.

The Mars Pathfinder mission proved that space exploration didn't have to be as expensive as it had been in the past. Engineers had devised unique ways to make the mission simple and inexpensive. Their hard work paid off in a big way as a new generation of young people was introduced to the wonder and excitement of space.

was 4 feet (1.2 meters) long. Its mission was to orbit 63 feet (19 meters) above the lunar surface for a year, measuring the moon's magnetic field and composition. One of its chief jobs was to determine if water ice is present at the moon's north and south poles.

Two months after it began orbiting the moon, Lunar Prospector sent back data indicating that there is almost certainly water ice present. A neutron spectrometer aboard the spacecraft found evidence of between 2 and 26 billion gallons (between 7 and 98 billion liters) of water. It is in the form of ice mixed with lunar soil and covers thousands of square miles, mostly at the moon's north pole.

The presence of ice is very valuable for a future space colony. Water, which is difficult to transport because of its weight, could be used to grow crops and generate power and air. In addition, water could be separated into hydrogen and oxygen and made into rocket fuel. The moon could become a kind of lunar filling station for further space travel.

NASA has plans to launch dozens of small probes in the next decades. Among them will be Stardust, which will make a 242-million-mile (390-million-kilometer) journey to Comet Wild-2. As the probe passes through the path of the comet, it will extend an arm that resembles a flyswatter. Ice and dust will be captured by the arm and returned to Earth seven years later for analysis.

In the summer of 2003, the Champollion/Deep Space 4 probe is set to lift off. It will travel about 233 million miles (375 million kilometers) from Earth to

Comet Tempel 1. A harpoon will be fired at the comet to anchor the spacecraft, and then a drill will collect a sample of the comet's core.

While probes are exploring the far reaches of space, NASA will also be busy with the construction of the International Space Station (ISS). The United States and fifteen other countries are partners in the space-station

This is a computer artist's concept of the completed International Space Station. Already under way, the construction of the station will be completed in space.

Astronaut Buzz Aldrin poses next to the American flag, which he and Neil Armstrong planted during their historic lunar landing in 1969. Their Lunar Module, the *Eagle*, is at the left side of the picture. Thirty years later, the flag still flies on the moon.

project. The assembly program was to begin in 1998 when the first section would be placed into orbit by Russia, the country that made up most of the former Soviet Union. Called *Zarya*, which is Russian for sunrise, the module contains the future station's propulsion systems, communications equipment, power generators, and life-support systems.

Additional modules will be added until the space station is complete. The last assembly flight is scheduled for May 2002. Countries involved in the project are Belgium, Brazil, Canada, Denmark, France, Germany, Italy, Japan, the Netherlands, Norway, Russia, Spain, Sweden, Switzerland, the United Kingdom, and the United States.

Phase I of the space-station program began in 1995, when American astronauts began living and working aboard the Russian space station Mir. Launched in 1986, Mir has been occupied continuously since that time by a series of Russian cosmonauts. The Mir missions gave American astronauts an opportunity to work in space for long periods of time. They also helped to build a bond of cooperation between two countries that were once enemies.

Phases II and III of the International Space Station are its assembly in space. The individual parts are too large to be connected on Earth and then sent into space, so the construction must take place in orbit. At least 800 hours of space walks by astronauts and cosmonauts will be needed to put the modules together.

Once the space station is completed, many scientific experiments and observations will be possible from the orbiting laboratory. Crystals grown in weightlessness

Index